Do You Like Building Things?

T0062046

Diane Lindsey Reeves

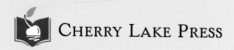
CHERRY LAKE PRESS

Published in the United States of America by Cherry Lake Publishing Group
Ann Arbor, Michigan
www.cherrylakepublishing.com

Reading Adviser: Beth Walker Gambro, MS, Ed., Reading Consultant, Yorkville, IL

Photo Credits: cover: © Panumas Yanuthai/Shutterstock; page 5: © Besjunior/Shutterstock; page 6: © CREATISTA/Shutterstock; page 7: © Monkey Business Images/Shutterstock; page 8: Navy Seaman Jennifer M. Kirkman/U.S. Department of Defense; page 9: Margo Wright/U.S. Air Force; page 10: © Rawpixel.com/Shutterstock; page 11: © sirtravelalot/Shutterstock; page 12: © Monkey Business Images/Shutterstock; page 13: © Gorodenkoff/Shutterstock; page 14: © SeventyFour/Shutterstock; page 15: © Bangkok Click Studio/Shutterstock; page 16: Hawaiian Volcano Observatory/U.S. Geological Survey; page 17: Andrew Stevens/USGS Pacific Coastal and Marine Science Center; page 18: Bureau of Safety and Environmental Enforcement/U.S. Department of the Interior; page 19: © kckate16/Shutterstock; page 20: © Nor Gal/Shutterstock; page 21: © Dmytro Zinkevych/Shutterstock; page 22: © Dwight Smith/Shutterstock; page 23: Navy Seaman Alexander Williams/US Department of Defense page 24: © BearFotos/Shutterstock; page 25: © Vadim Ratnikov/Shutterstock; page 26: © fotoNino/Shutterstock; page 27: © DC Studio/Shutterstock; page 30: © Nestor Rizhniak/Shutterstock; page 31: © Just dance/Shutterstock

Cherry Lake Press is an imprint of Cherry Lake Publishing Group.

Library of Congress Cataloging-in-Publication Data

Names: Reeves, Diane Lindsey, 1959- author.
Title: Do you like building things? / by Diane Lindsey Reeves.
Description: Ann Arbor, Michigan : Cherry Lake Publishing, [2023] | Series: Career clues for kids | Includes bibliographical references and index. | Audience: Grades 4-6
Summary: "Do you like putting things together and building? That might be a potential clue to your future career! This book explores what a career in building might look like. Readers will discover how their interests can lead to a lifelong future career. Aligned to curriculum standards and 21st Century Skills, Career Clues for Kids prepares readers for a successful future. Includes table of contents, glossary, index, sidebars, and author biographies" — Provided by publisher.
Identifiers: LCCN 2022039261 | ISBN 9781668919439 (hardcover) | ISBN 9781668920459 (paperback) | ISBN 9781668923115 (pdf) | ISBN 9781668921784 (ebook)
Subjects: LCSH: Building—Vocational guidance—Juvenile literature. | Building trades—Vocational guidance—Juvenile literature. | Construction workers—Vocational guidance—Juvenile literature.
Classification: LCC TH159 .R44 2023 | DDC 690.023—dc23/eng/20221012
LC record available at https://lccn.loc.gov/2022039261

Cherry Lake Publishing Group would like to acknowledge the work of the Partnership for 21st Century Learning, a Network of Battelle for Kids. Please visit *http://www.battelleforkids.org/networks/p21* for more information.

Printed in the United States of America
Corporate Graphics

Diane Lindsey Reeves likes to write books that help students figure out what they want to be when they grow up. She mostly lives in Washington, D.C., but spends as much time as she can in North Carolina and South Carolina with her grandkids.

CONTENTS

Building a Cool Career

Figuring out what you want to be when you grow up can be tricky. There are so many choices! How are you supposed to know which one to pick? Here's an idea... follow the clues!

The fact that you are reading a book called *Do You Like Building Things?* is your first clue. It suggests that you have an interest in building stuff. True? If so, start looking at careers you can build a future on!

Your **interests** say a lot about who you are and what makes you tick. What do you like doing best?

Abilities are things that you are naturally good at doing. Another word for ability is talent. Everyone has natural talents and abilities. Some are more obvious than others. What are you really good at doing?

Curiosity offers up other career clues. To succeed in any career, you have to learn what it takes to do that job. You may have to go to college or trade school. It means gaining new skills and getting experience. Curiosity about a subject keeps you at it until you become an expert. What do you want to know more about?

Interests. Abilities. Curiosity. These clues can help you find a career that's right for you.

FIND THE CLUES!

Each chapter includes several clues about careers you might enjoy.

INTERESTS: **What do you like doing?**

ABILITIES: **What are you good at doing?**

CURIOSITY: **What do you want to learn more about?**

Are You a Future Builder?

WOULD YOU ENJOY...

Looking under the hood of a turbo jet engine? (see page 8)

Designing cool places for people to hang out? (see page 10)

Taking cars of the future for a spin? (see page 12)

Making furniture, houses, and more? (see page 14)

Helping people find their way around the world?
(see page 16)

Planning new roads, airports, tunnels, and bridges?
(see page 18)

Inventing new products that solve problems? (see page 20)

Building big structures like bridges? (see page 22)

Working outdoors to create green spaces? (see page 24)

Rethinking cities of the future? (see page 26)

READ ON FOR MORE CLUES ABOUT BUILDING CAREERS!

Aircraft Mechanic

A person who repairs and services airplanes and helicopters.

Aircraft mechanics get airplanes and helicopters ready to fly. Sometimes they service aircraft between flights at an airport. There is a long list of parts and systems to check and not much time! Every little detail is a big deal when it comes to safety. Some aircraft mechanics work on major repairs in huge airplane **hangars**. Many aircraft mechanics get their training in the military. Can you imagine fixing a fighter jet on an **aircraft carrier** in the middle of an ocean?

CLUES!

INTEREST: **Airplanes**

ABILITY: **Fixing things**

CURIOSITY: **How airplanes work**

INVESTIGATE!

NOW: **Make a paper airplane that flies fast and far.**

LATER: **Get special training at a trade school
or in the military.**

Architect

A person who designs buildings.

Architects design the places where people live, work, and play. This includes your house, school, and the places where your parents work. It also includes the places where you like to have fun, like sports stadiums and theaters. Architects are part artist and part scientist. They use creative talent to design cool spaces that look good. They use science skills to design safe spaces that work well. Architects need good people skills to explore ideas with clients. They work with builders and engineers to turn their ideas into real places.

CLUES!

INTEREST: Cool buildings

ABILITY: Putting together Lego kits

CURIOSITY: How buildings are made

INVESTIGATE!

NOW: Don't leave home without a sketchpad and pencil!

LATER: Earn a college degree in architecture.

Automotive Engineer

A person who designs and improves cars.

Many years ago, cars replaced horses and buggies. Who knew that it was the start of all kinds of cool careers? Like automotive engineers! Automotive engineers imagine new looks and features for cars. This includes everything from body styles and seatbelts to headlights and paint colors. Every year it's a challenge to design cars that are better than the year before. A big focus is on developing smarter cars. Think **hybrid cars** and driverless cars! Their goal is to develop safe cars that do not rely on **fossil fuels**.

CLUES!

INTEREST: Car makes and models

ABILITY: Building model cars

CURIOSITY: How cars look and work

INVESTIGATE!

NOW: Draw a picture of the car you hope to drive someday.

LATER: Earn an automotive engineering degree in college.

Carpenter

A person who builds and repairs things made out of wood.

Some carpenters repair or install **foundations**. They build walls, roofs, windows, and doors. This type of work is called rough carpentry. Others, called woodworkers, make things like kitchen cabinets, furniture, and even musical instruments. This type of work is called finish carpentry. Both types require lots of practice and on-the-job learning. All must know how to follow plans, work with lots of tools, and measure accurately.

CLUES!

INTEREST: Adding to your tool collection

ABILITY: Making things with tools

CURIOSITY: Woodworking

INVESTIGATE!

NOW: Build a birdhouse. You can find instructions online.

LATER: Graduate high school and apprentice with a construction company or union.

Cartographer

A person who creates maps.

Early cartographers used the stars to chart their maps. The earliest known maps were carved into stone. Today cartographers use data collected from satellites in outer space. They also use all kinds of technology. Think lasers attached to airplanes to map out Earth's **topography**! Sometimes they do field work where they **survey** land and take photos. Growing use of the global positioning system (GPS) is expected to create opportunities for future cartographers.

CLUES!

INTEREST: **Google maps**

ABILITY: **Having a good sense of direction**

CURIOSITY: **How GPS satellites work**

INVESTIGATE!

NOW: **Draw a map showing ways to get from your house to your school.**

LATER: **Earn a college degree in cartography, geography, or surveying.**

Civil Engineer

A person who designs and supervises the building of big structures.

Civil engineers work on the systems and spaces that keep a city running smoothly. This includes all the places communities share. Civil engineers play a role in building new neighborhoods, office buildings, roads, bridges, and more. Civil engineers are problem-solvers. They use strong math and science skills to tackle big issues like transportation, pollution, and water supply. They divide their time between offices and job sites. At the office, they use computers to develop complex plans. They put those plans into action at job sites.

CLUES!

INTEREST: Bridges and skyscrapers

ABILITY: Thinking creatively

CURIOSITY: All things math and science

INVESTIGATE!

NOW: Use straws or toothpicks to build a bridge that can hold a certain amount of weight.

LATER: Earn a college degree in civil engineering.

Industrial Designer

A person who solves business problems by creating products and experiences.

Industrial designers design products that are manufactured for people to buy. Some design toys or bicycles. Some design smartphones or TVs. Others work on furniture, fabrics, or sporting goods. No matter the product, industrial designers always start with an idea. They use computer-aided design (CAD) software to sketch out their ideas. They may even use a 3D printer to create models of their ideas. Their work is part creative, part business, and part engineering.

CLUES!

INTEREST: New gadgets and technologies

ABILITY: Brainstorming good ideas

CURIOSITY: How to use computer-aided design (CAD)

INVESTIGATE!

NOW: Start an idea notebook.

LATER: Earn a college degree in industrial design, fine arts, or graphic design.

Ironworker/Welder

A person who installs iron and steel to form and support buildings.

Human bodies have bones to hold them together. Buildings, bridges, and roads have iron and steel frames. Ironworkers are the skilled tradespeople who put these supports in place. Structural ironworkers connect steel columns and **girders** for tall structures like skyscrapers and bridges. Ironworkers use different types of tools to cut and shape the iron and steel. Then they weld or bolt it into place. Will a structure stand or fall? It depends on ironworkers doing a good job!

CLUES!

INTEREST: **Working outdoors**

ABILITY: **Using an Erector Set to build models**

CURIOSITY: **How bridges and skyscrapers work**

INVESTIGATE!

NOW: **Work out and get in shape. This job requires muscle!**

LATER: **Graduate high school and apprentice at a local ironworker training center.**

Landscaper

A person who designs and maintains gardens and other outdoor spaces.

The next time you visit a park, notice all the green and growing things. All that beauty starts in the mind of a landscaper. Landscapers design gardens and outdoor spaces for homes and public places. They plant, install, and maintain these areas to keep them looking good. Landscaping is a great gig for people who enjoy working outdoors. It helps if they don't mind getting their hands dirty!

CLUES!

INTERESTS: Nature hikes

ABILITIES: Taking care of plants

CURIOSITY: How green things grow

INVESTIGATE!

NOW: Create a container garden for your bedroom windowsill.

LATER: Get experience with a landscaping company.

Urban Planner

A person who creates plans and programs for the use of land.

Every city needs homes to live in and schools to learn in. They need businesses for work. Don't forget places to play! It's an urban planner's job to make sure their city has a good mix of all these things. Sometimes this means planning new neighborhoods. Other times it means improving what's already there. The focus now is on smart cities. Smart cities are good for people and good for planet Earth.

CLUES!

INTERESTS: Video games like Minecraft and SimCity

ABILITIES: Thinking visually

CURIOSITY: Eco-friendly communities

INVESTIGATE!

NOW: Notice what makes every city you visit unique.

LATER: Earn a college degree in urban planning.

Builders Workshop

Keep investigating your career clues until you find a career that's right for you! Here are more ways to explore.

Join a Club

Ask your teacher or school counselor about STEM or engineering clubs at your school or in your community.

Talk to People with Interesting Careers

Ask your teacher or parent to help you connect with someone who has a career like the one you want. Be ready to ask lots of questions!

Volunteer

Help build houses for families who need them.

Find out more at:
https://www.habitat.org/volunteer/near-you/youth-programs

Enjoy Career Day

School career days can be a great way to find out more about different careers. Make the most of this opportunity.

Explore Online

With adult supervision, use your favorite search engine to look online for information about careers you are interested in.

Participate in Take Your Daughters and Sons to Work Day

Every year on the fourth Thursday of April, kids all over the world go to work with their parents or other trusted adults to find out what the world of work is really like.

Find out more at: https://daughtersandsonstowork.org

Resources

Airplane Mechanic
NASA: What is Aeronautics?
https://www.grc.nasa.gov/www/k-12/UEET/StudentSite/aeronautics.html

Architecture
archKIDecture
https://archkidecture.org

Automotive Engineer
DK FindOut! The History of Cars
https://www.dkfindout.com/us/transportation/history-cars

Carpenter
Build Your Future: Construction Careers
https://byf.org/explore/construction-careers

Cartographer
Kids World Atlas
National Geographic. *Kids World Atlas.* Washington, DC: National Geographic Kids, 2021.

Civil Engineer
The Way Things Work Now
Macauley, David. *The Way Things Work Now.* Boston, MA: Houghton Mifflin Harcourt, 2016.

Industrial Designer
Industrial Design
Mooney, Carla. *Industrial Design: Why Smart Phones Aren't Round and Other Scientific Mysteries for Kids.* Norwich, VT: Nomad Press, 2018.

Ironworker/Welder
How Stuff Works: How Skyscrapers Work
https://science.howstuffworks.com/engineering/structural/skyscraper.htm

Landscaper
History of Central Park
https://www.centralparknyc.org/park-history

Urban Planner
16 Most Famous Cities in the U.S.
https://heyexplorer.com/famous-cities-in-the-us

Glossary

abilities (uh-BIH-luh-teez) natural talents or acquired skills

aircraft carrier (AYR-kraft KER-ee-uhr) large warship serving as a base for aircraft that can take off and land on its deck

apprentice (uh-PREN-tuhs) to learn a job or skill by assisting an experienced worker

curiosity (kyur-ee-AH-suh-tee) a strong desire to know or learn about something

fossil fuels (FAH-suhl FYOOLZ) fuels such as coal, oil, and natural gas that are made from decomposing plants and animals

foundations (fown-DAY-shuhns) solid structures on which buildings are constructed

girders (GUHR-duhrz) large iron or steel beams used to build bridges and large buildings

hangars (HANG-uhrs) large buildings in which aircraft are kept and repaired

hybrid car (HYE-bruhd KAHR) car with both a gasoline engine and an electric motor

interests (IN-tuh-ruhsts) things or activities that a person enjoys or is concerned about

survey (suhr-VAY) to examine and measure a piece of land

topography (tuh-PAH-gruh-fee) detailed description of the physical features of an area, including hills, valleys, and rivers

Index